PYTHON CRASH COURSE

A COMPLETE BEGINNER'S GUIDE TO LEARN PYTHON AND CODING QUICKLY

MARK MATTHES AND ERIC LUTZ

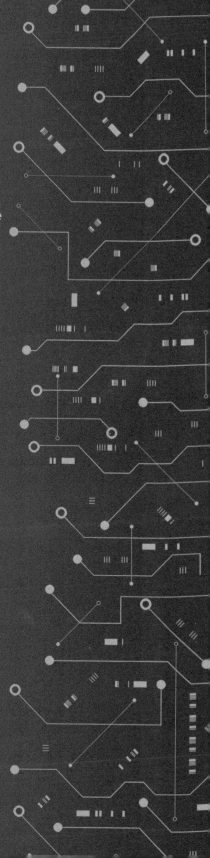

TABLE OF CONTENTS

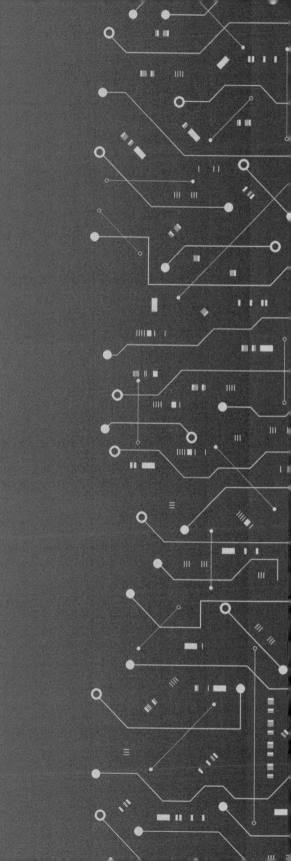

INTRODUCTION

The introduction of technologies, especially computers, has influenced our behavior differently. Some people spend most of their time on computers that create programs and websites to make a living, while others mess around with computers to try to understand many different things about how machines work. Programming is one of the areas in networks that most people in the world focus on as a source of income. They can work in a company or computer repair to protect computers from attacks such as hackers or viruses.

However, nothing is easy when it comes to computer technology. Before working on a computer program, it is essential that you focus more on the basic things, including the correct codes and language, as this will allow you to deliver the correct program. With the availability of many cording creation options such as C ++, Python and Java, you can choose a method that you are expert in and that will also facilitate your work. In this book, we will focus on Python and why it is good than other programming languages.

One of the most advanced programming tools is Python because anyone, including beginners or experts, can easily use and read it. The secret to using Python is that you can read it because it contains syntax, which allows you as a programmer to express your concepts without necessarily creating a coding page. This is what makes Python easier to use and read than the other codes, including C ++ and Java. Overall, Python is the best language for you because of its usability and readability. We are therefore confident that it will be easy for you to read and understand all the codes you enter while creating your first program during and after this course.

Features of the Python

Python has the following characteristics:

• Large library: it works with other programming projects such as searching for texts, connecting to the web servers and exchanging files.

• Interactive: Using the Python is very simple because you can easily test codes to determine if they work.

• It is free software; so you can always download it from the internet with your computer.

• Python programming language can be extended

to other modules such as C ++ and C.

• Has an elegant syntax that makes it easy for beginners to read and use.

• Has several basic data types to choose from.

History of the Python

Python programming was discovered by Guido Van Rossum in 1989 while he was carrying out a project at the Dutch research institute CWI, but it was later discontinued. Guido has successfully used a number of basic languages, the so-called ABC language, to work on the Python. According to Van Rossum, the strength of the python language is that you can either keep it simple or extend it to more platforms to support many platforms at once. The design allowed the system to communicate with the libraries and various file formats easily.

Since its introduction, many programmers now use Python in the world, and in fact, many tools are included to improve operation and efficiency. Many programmers have taken various initiatives to educate everyone about using python programming language and how it can help ease the fear of complex computer codes.

However, the Python was made open source by Van Rossum a few years ago to allow all programmers access and even make changes to it. This has changed a lot in the field of programming. For example, there was a release of the Python 2.0.

Python 2.0 was community-oriented, making it transparent in the development process. While many people don't use Python, there are still some programmers and organizations that use part of the version.

The Python 3, a unique version, was released in 2008. Although the version has many different functions, it is completely different from the first two versions and it is not easy to update the program. While this version is not backwards compatible, it has a small creator to show what needs to be changed when uploading the files.

Why you should use Python

There are many types of computer coding programs in the world, each with its advantages and disadvantages. However, Python has proven to be the best option for a variety of reasons, such as readability, and can be used on many platforms without changing things. Using Python has the following advantages;

• Readability

Since it is designed in the English language, a beginner will find it easy to read and us. There are also a number of rules that help the programmer understand how to format everything, and this makes it easy for a programmer to create a simple code that other people can follow when using their projects with it.

- Community

Today, there are many workshops for Python worldwide. A beginner can visit online, offline or both to learn more or even seek clarification on Python. Also, online and offline workshops can improve your understanding of Python, as well as your socialization skills. It is best for the personal computer as it works successfully on many different platforms. In fact, all beginners find it easy to code or learn from the expert.

- Libraries

For over 25 years, programmers have been using Python to teach the beginners how to use different codes written with it. The system is very open to programmers and they can use the available codes indefinitely. In fact, a student can download and install the system and use it for their personal use, such as writing your codes and completing the product.

General terms in the Python

Understanding the standard terms used in Python is essential to you. It makes everything easy to know when you get started. Following are the most common terms in the Python programming language;

v Function: refers to a code block that is called when a programmer uses a calling program. The goal is also to provide free services and accurate calculation.

v Class: a template used for developing user-defined objects. It is friendly and easy to use by everyone including the beginners.

Ver Immutable: refers to an object with a fixed value and is contained within the code. These can be numbers, strings, or tuples. Such an object cannot be changed.

St Docstring: Refers to a string that is displayed in the function, class definition, and module. This object is always available in the documentation tools.

v List: refers to the data type built into the Python and contains values sorted. Such values include strings and numbers.

LE IDLE: Stands for an integrated development environment that allows the users to type the code while interpreting and editing it in the same window. Best suited for beginners because it is an excellent example of code.

v Interactive: Python has become the most suitable programming language for beginners due to its interactive nature. As a beginner, you can try out many things in the IDLE (interpreter to see their response and effects).

Qu Triple Quoted String: The string helps an individual to have single and double quotes in the string, making it easy to go through different lines of code.

v Object: it refers to all data in a state such as attitudes, methods, defined behaviors or values.

Type: refers to a group of data categories in the programming language and differences in properties, functions and methods.

Tuple: Refers to the datatype built into the Python and is an unchanging set of values, although it contains some changeable values.

CHAPTER - 1

FUNCTIONS AND MODULES

Functions

Creating and calling a function is easy. The primary purpose of a function is to allow you to organize, simplify, and modularize your code. Whenever you have a set of code that you will need to execute in sequence from time to time, defining a function for that set of code will save you time and space in your program. Instead of repeatedly typing code or even copy pasting, you simply define a function.

We began with almost no prior knowledge about Python except for a clue that it was some kind of programming language that is in great demand these days. Now, look at you; creating simple programs, executing codes and fixing small-scale problems on your own. Not bad at all! However, learning always comes to a point where things can get rather trickier.

In quite a similar fashion, Functions are docile looking things; you call them when you need to get something done. But did you know that these functions have so much going on at the back? Imagine every function as a mini-program. It is also written by programmers like us to carry out specific things without having us to write lines and lines of codes. You only do it once, save it as a function and then just call the function where it is applicable or needed.

The time has come for us to dive into a complex world of functions where we don't just learn how to use them effectively, but we also look into what goes on behind these functions, and how we can come up with our very own personalized function. This will be slightly challenging, but I promise, there are more references that you will enjoy to keep the momentum going.

How to define and call function?

To start, we need to take a look at how we are able to define our own functions in this language. The function in Python is going to be defined when we use the statement of "def" and then follow it with a function name and some parentheses in place as well. This lets the compiler know that you are defining a function, and which function you would like to define at this time as well. There are going to be a few rules in place when it comes to defining one of these functions though, and it is important to do these in the proper manner to ensure your code acts in the way that you would like. Some of the Python rules that we need to follow for defining these functions will include:

1. Any of the arguments or input parameters that you would like to use have to be placed within the parentheses so that the compiler knows what is going on.

2. The function first statement is something that can be an optional statement something like a documentation string that goes with your function if needed.

3. The code that is found within all of the functions that we are working with needs to start out with a colon, and then we need to indent it as well.

4. The statement return that we get, or the expression, will need to exit a function at this time. We can then have the option of passing back a value to the caller. A return statement that doesn't have an argument with it is going to give us the same return as none.

Before we get too familiar with some of the work that can be done with these Python functions, we need to take some time to understand the rules of indentation when we are declaring these functions in Python. The same kinds of rules are going to be applicable to some of the other elements of Python as well, such as declaring conditions, variables, and loops, so learning how this work can be important here.

Float

This function is used to convert a value to a floating point number. Recall that a floating point value is simply a decimal number. Let's look at an example of this function.

The following program showcases the float function.

```
# This program looks at string functions

a=1

print(a)

print(float(a))
```

This program's output will be as follows:

1

1.0

Modules

What are the Modules?

In Python, a module is a portion of a program (an extension file) that can be invoked through other programs without having to write them in every program used. Besides, they can define classes and variables. These modules contain related sentences between them and can be used at any time. The use of the modules is based on using a code (program body, functions, variables) already stored on it called import. With the use of the modules, it can be observed that Python allows simplifying the programs a lot because it allows us to simplify the problems into a smaller one to make the code shorter so that programmers do not get lost when looking for something in hundreds of coding lines when making codes.

How to Create a Module?

To create a module in Python, we don't need a lot; it's very simple.

For example: if you want to create a module that prints a city, we write our code in the editor and save it as "mycity.py".

Once this is done, we will know that this will be the name of our module (omitting the .py sentence), which will be assigned to the global variable __ city__.

But, beyond that, we can see that the file "mycity.py" is pretty simple and not complicated at all, since the only thing inside is a function called "print_city" which will have a string as a parameter, and what it will do is to print "Hello, welcome to", and this will concatenate with the string that was entered as a parameter.

Importing Modules

The keyword import is used to import.

Example

Import first

The dot operator can help us access a function as long as we know the name of the module.

Example

Start IDLE.

Navigate to the File menu and click New Window.

Type the following:

```
first.add(6,8)
```

CHAPTER - 2

DEFINING YOUR OWN FUNCTIONS

Python functions are a good way of organizing the structure of our code. The functions can be used for grouping sections of code that are related. The work of functions in any programming language is to improve the modularity of code and make it possible to reuse code.

Python comes with many in-built functions. A good example of such a function is the "print()" function which we use for displaying the contents on the screen. Despite this, it is possible for us to create our own functions in Python. Such functions are referred to as the "user-defined functions".

To define a function, we use the "def" keyword which is then followed by the name of the function, and then the parenthesis (()).

The parameters or the input arguments have to be placed inside the parenthesis. The parameters can also be defined within parenthesis. The function has a body or the code block and this must begin with a colon (:) and it has to be indented. It is good for you to note that the default setting is that the arguments have a positional behavior. This means that they should be passed while following the order in which you defined them.

Example:

```python
#!/usr/bin/python3
def functionExample():
    print('The function code to run')
    bz = 10 + 23
    print(bz)
```

We have defined a function named functionExample. The parameters of a function are like the variables for the function. The parameters are usually added inside the parenthesis, but our above function has no parameters. When you run above code, nothing will happen since we simply defined the function and specified what it should do. The function can be called as shown below:

```python
#!/usr/bin/python3
```

```python
def functionExample():

    print('The function code to run')

    bz = 10 + 23

functionExample()

It will print this:
```

The function code to run

That is how we can have a basic Python function.

Function Parameters

You can dynamically define arguments for a function. Example:

```python
#!/usr/bin/python3

def additionFunction(n1,n2):

    result = n1 + n2

    print('The first number is', n1)

    print('The second number is', n2)

    print("The sum is", result)

additionFunction(10,5)
```

The code returns the following result:

```
The first number is 10
The second number is 5
The sum is 15
```

We defined a function named addFunction. The function takes two parameters namely n1 and n2. We have another variable named result which is the sum of the two function parameters. In the last statement, we have called the function and passed the values for the two parameters. The function will calculate the value of variable result by adding the two numbers. We finally get the result shown above.

Note that during our function definition, we specified two parameters, n1 and n2. Try to call the function will either more than two parameters, or 1 parameter and see what happens. Example:

```python
#!/usr/bin/python3

def additionFunction(n1,n2):

    result = n1 + n2

    print('The first number is', n1)

    print('The second number is', n2)
```

```
    print("The sum is", result)

additionFunction(5)
```

In the last statement in our code above, we have passed only one argument to the function, that is, 5. The program gives an error when executed:

```
Traceback (most recent call last):
  File "main.py", line 9, in
    additionFunction(5)
TypeError: additionFunction() missing 1 required positional argument: 'n2'
```

The error message simply tells us one argument is missing. What if we run it with more than two arguments?

```
#!/usr/bin/python3

def additionFunction(n1,n2):

    result = n1 + n2

    print('The first number is', n1)

    print('The second number is', n2)

    print("The sum is", result)

additionFunction(5,10,9)
```

We also get an error message:

```
File "main.py", line 9, in
    additionFunction(5,10,9)
TypeError: additionFunction() takes 2 positional arguments but 3 were given
```

The error message tells us the function expects two arguments but we have passed 3 to it.

In most programming languages, parameters to a function can be passed either by reference or by value. Python supports parameter passing only by reference. This means if what the parameter refers to is changed in the function; the same change will also be reflected in the calling function. Example:

```python
#!/usr/bin/python3

def referenceFunction(ls1):

    print ("List values before change: ", ls1)

    ls1[0]=800

    print ("List values after change: ", ls1)

    return

# Calling the function

ls1 = [940,1209,6734]

referenceFunction( ls1 )

print ("Values outside function: ", ls1)
```

The code gives this result:

```
List values before change:  [940, 1209, 6734]
List values after change:   [800, 1209, 6734]
Values outside function:    [800, 1209, 6734]
```

What we have done in this example is that we have maintained the reference of the objects which are being passed and then values have been appended to the same function.

In next example below, we are passing by reference then the same reference will be overwritten inside the same function which has been called:

```
#!/usr/bin/python3

def referenceFunction( ls1 ):

    ls1 = [11,21,31,41]

    print ("Values inside the function: ", ls1)

    return

ls1 = [51,91,81]

referenceFunction( ls1 )

print ("Values outside function: ", ls1)
```

The code gives this result:

```
Values inside the function:  [11, 21, 31, 41]
Vlaues outside function:  [51, 91, 81]
```

Note that the "ls1" parameter will be local to the function "referenceFunction". Even if this is changed within the function, the "ls1" will not be affected in any way. As the output shows above, the function helps us achieve nothing.

Function Parameter Defaults

There are default parameters for functions, which the function creator can use in his or her functions. This means that one has the choice of using the default parameters, or even using the ones they need to use by specifying them. To use the default parameters, the parameters having defaults are expected to be last ones written in function parameters. Example:

```
#!/usr/bin/python3

def myFunction(n1, n2=6):

    pass
```

In above example, the parameter n2 has been given a default value unlike parameter n1. The parameter n2 has been written as the last one in the function parameters. The values for such a function may be accessed as follows:

```
#!/usr/bin/python3
def windowFunction(width,height,font='TNR'):
    # printing everything
    print(width,height,font)
windowFunction(245,278)
```

The code outputs the following:

```
245 278 TNR
```

The parameter font had been given a default value, that is, TNR. In the last line of the above code, we have passed only two parameters to the function, that is, the values for width and height parameters. However, after calling the function, it returned the values for the three parameters. This means for a parameter with default, we don't need to specify its value or even mention it when calling the function.

However, it's still possible for you to specify the value for the parameter during function call. You can specify a different value to what had been specified as the default and you will get the new one as value of the parameter. Example:

```python
#!/usr/bin/python3
def windowFunction(width,height,font='TNR'):
    # printing everything
    print(width,height,font)
windowFunction(245,278,'GEO')
```

The program outputs this:

```
245 278 GEO
```

Above, the value for parameter was given the default value "TNR". When calling the function in the last line of the code, we specified a different value for this parameter, which is "GEO". The code returned the value as "GEO". The default value was overridden.

CHAPTER - 3

WORKING WITH YOUR OWN MODULE

Modules, also known as packages, are a set of names. This is usually a library of functions and object classes that are made available to be used within different programs. In order to use modules in a Python program, the following statements are used: import, from, reload. The first one imports the whole module. The second allows import only a specific name or element from the module. The third one, reload, allows reloading a code of a module while Python is running and without stopping in it. Before digging into their definition and development, let's start first by the utility of modules or packages within Python.

Modules Concept and Utility within Python

Modules are a very simple way to make a system component organized. Basically, modules allow reusing the same code over and over. So far, we were working in a Python interactive session.

Every code we have written and tested is lost once we exit the interactive session. Modules are saved in files that make them persistent, reusable, and sharable. You can consider modules as a set of files where you can define functions, names, data objects, attributes, and so on. Modules are a tool to group several components of a system in a single place. In Python programming, modules are among the highest-level unit. They point to the name of packages and tools. In addition, they allow the sharing of the implemented data.

You only need one copy of the module to be able to use across a large program. If an object is to be used in different functions and programs, coding it as a module allows share it with other programmers.

To have a sense of the architecture of Python coding, we go through some general structure explanation. We have been using so far in this book very simple code examples that do not really have high-level structure. In large applications, a program is a set of several Python files. By Python files, we mean files that contain Python code and have a .py extension. There is one main high-level program and the other files are the modules. The high-level file consists of the main code that dictates the control flow and executes the application. Module files define the tools that are needed to process elements and components of the main program and maybe elsewhere. The main program makes use of the tools that are specified in the modules.

In their turn, modules make use of tools that are specified in other modules. When you import a module in Python, you have access to every tool that is declared or defined in that specific module. Attributes are the variables or the functions associated with the tools within a module. Hence, when a module is imported, we have access to the attributes of the tools as well to process them. For instance, let's consider we have two Python files named file1.py and file2.py where the file1.py is the main program and file2.py is the module.

In order to use this function in the main program, we should define code statements in the file1.py as follows:

```
Import file2

A = file2.Xfactorial (3)
```

The first line imports the module file2.py. This statement means to load the file file2.py. This gives access to the file1.py to all tools and functions defined in file2.py by the name file2. The function Xfactorial is called by the second line. The module file2.py is where this function is defined using the attributes' syntax. The line file2.Xfactorial() means fetch any name value of Xfactorial and lies within the code body of file2. In this example, it is a function that is callable. So, we have provided an input argument and assigned the output result to the variable A. If we add a third statement to print the variable A and run the file file1.py, it would display 6 which is the factorial of 3. Along Python, you will see the attribute syntax as object.attribute. This basically allows calling the attributes that might be a function or data object that provides properties of the object.

Note that some modules that you might import when programming with Python are available in Python itself. As we have mentioned at the beginning of this book, Python comes with a standard large library that has built-in modules. These modules support all common tasks that might be needed in programming from operating system interfaces to graphical user interface. They are not part of the language. However, they can be imported and comes with a software installation package. You can check the complete list of available modules in a manual that comes with the installation or goes to the official Python website: www.Python.org. This manual is kept updated every time a new version of Python is released.

CHAPTER - 4

WORKING WITH FILES

The data can be stored using either a database or a file. The database maintains the integrity and relevance of the data and makes the data safer and more reliable. Using files to store data is very simple and easy to use, and there is no need to install database management systems and other operating environments.

Files are usually used to store application software parameters or temporary data. Python's file operation is very similar to Java's file operation. Python provides modules such as os and os.path to process files.

Files and streams

Common Operation of Files

Files are usually used to store data or application system parameters. Python provides os, os.path, shutil, and other modules to process files, including functions such as opening files, reading and writing files, copying and deleting files.

Creation of Files

In Python3, the global file () function has been removed, and the open () function has been retained. The function open () can be used to open or create files. This function can specify the processing mode and set the open file to read-only, write-only, or read-write status.

The declaration of open () is as follows:

```
open(file, mode='r', buffering=-1,
encoding=None,

errors=None, newline=None,
closefd=Trueopener=None) -> file object

[Code Description]
```

The parameter file is the name of the opened file. If the file does not exist, open () creates a file named name and then opens the file. The parameter mode refers to the open mode of the file. Parameter buffering sets the cache mode. 0 means no cache; 1 indicates line buffering. If it is greater than 1, it indicates the size of the buffer, in bytes.

Here, open () returns a file object, which can perform various operations on the file.

Opening Mode of Files notes that "B" mode must be used for reading and writing files such as pictures and videos.

The file class is used for file management. It can create, open, read and write, close files, etc.

File processing is generally divided into the following 3 steps:

1) Create and open a file and use the file () function to return a file object.

2) Call read (), write () and other methods of the file object to process the file.

3) Call close () to close the file and release the resources occupied by the file object.

Note that the close () method is necessary. Although Python provides a garbage collection mechanism to clean up objects that are no longer used, it is a good habit to release resources that are no longer needed manually. It also explicitly tells Python's garbage collector that the object needs to be cleaned.

The following code demonstrates the creation, writing, and closing of files.

```
01 # Create File

02 context='''This is countryside'''
```

```
03 f=open('rod.txt', 'w') # open file

04 f.write(context) # write string to file

Close () # close file

[Code Description]
```

The third line of code calls open () to create the file hello.txt and sets the access mode of the file to "W." Open () returns file object f.

The fourth line of code writes the value of the variable context into the file hello.txt

Line 5 calls the close () method of object f to release the resources occupied by object f.

Reading of Text Files

There are many ways to read a file. You can use readline (), readlines (), or Read () functions to read a file. The implementation method of reading files by these functions will be introduced one by one.

1. readline ()

Readline () reads one line of the file at a time, and the file needs to be read cyclically using a permanent true expression. However, when the file pointer moves to the end of the file, there will be an error reading the file using readline (). Therefore, a judgment statement needs to be added to the program to judge whether the file pointer moves to the end of the file, and the loop is interrupted by the statement. The following code demonstrates the use of readline ().

```
01 # Use readline () to Read Files
02 f=open("rod.txt")
03 while True:
04 line=f.readline()
05 if line:
06 print (line)
07 else:
08 break
09 f.close()
[Code Description]
```

The code in line 3 uses "True" as the loop condition to form a permanent true loop.

Line 4 calls readline () to read every line of the hello. txt file. Each cycle outputs the following results in turn.

This is countryside

Line 5 code, judge whether the variable LINE is true. If true, the content of the current line is output; otherwise, exit the loop. If the fourth line of code is changed to the following statement, the reading method is slightly different, but the reading content is exactly the same.

```
line=f.readline(2)
```

This line of code does not mean that only 2 bytes are read per line, but that each line reads 2 bytes at a time until the end of the line.

2. Multi-line reading method readlines ()

To read a file using readlines (), you need to return the elements in the list by looping through readlines (). The readlines () function reads multiple lines of data in a file at once.

The following code demonstrates how readlines () reads a file.

```
01 # use readlines () to read files
02 f=file('rod.txt')
03 lines=f.readlines()
04 for line in lines: # read multiple lines at once
05 print (line)
```

```
06 f.close()
```

[Code Description]

The third line of code calls readlines () to store all the contents of the file rod.txt in the list lines.

The fourth line of code loops through the contents of the list lines.

Line 5 code output list lines for each element

```
01 f=open("rod.txt")

02 context=f.read(5) # reads the first 5 bytes of
the file

03 print (context)

04 print (f.tell()) # returns the current pointer
position of the file object

05 context=f.read(5) # continue reading 5 bytes
of content

06 print (context)

07 print (f.tell()) # output file current pointer
position

08 f.close()
```

[Code Description]

The second line of code calls read(5) to read the contents of the first 5 bytes in the hello.txt file and store it in the variable context. At this point, the pointer of the file moves to the 5th byte.

The third line of code outputs the result of the variable context and the output is "hello."

Line 4 calls tell () to output the current file

Line 5 code calls read(5) again to read the contents of bytes 6 to 10.

The output of line 6 is "world."

Line 7 code outputs the current file pointer position: 10.

Note that the location of the file pointer will be recorded inside the file object for the next operation. As long as the file object does not execute the close () method, the file pointer will not be released.

Writing a Text File

The implementation of file writing also has many methods. You can use the write (), writelines () methods to write files. It uses the write () method to write strings to files, while the writelines () method can write the contents stored in the list to files.

The following code demonstrates how to write elements in the list to a file.

```
01 # use writelines () to write files
02 f=file("rod.txt," "w+")
03 li=["hello country side\n," "hello city\n"]
04 f.writelines(li)
05 f.close()
[Code Description]
```

The second line of code uses the "w+" mode to create and open the file hello.txt

Line 3 defines a list Li. Li stores 2 elements, each representing 1 line in the file, and "\n" is used for line feed.

The fourth line of code calls writelines () to write the contents of list li into the file.

The contents of the document are as follows.

hello countryside

hello City

The above two methods will erase the original contents of the file before writing and rewrite the new contents, which is equivalent to "overwriting." If you need to keep the original contents of the file and just add new contents, you can open the file using mode "a+."

The following code demonstrates the join operation of the file.

```
01 # Joins New Content to File

02 f=file("rod.txt," "first+") # is written by joining a+

03 new_context="It is over"

04 f.write(getdetails)

05 f.close()

[Code Description]
```

The second line of code uses the mode "first+" to open the file hello.txt

The fourth line of code calls the write () method, the original contents of the hello.txt file remain unchanged, and the contents of the variable getdetails are written to the end of the rod.txt file. Txt is as follows.

hello countryside

hello City

goodbye

Writing files using writelines () is faster. If there

are too many strings to write to a file, you can use writelines () to improve efficiency. If only a small number of strings need to be written, write () can be used directly.

Deleting Files

The deletion of files requires the use of os modules and os.path modules. Os module provides operating system-level interface functions for system environment, files, directories, etc. File Handling Functions Commonly Used in os Modules Note that the use of the OS module's open () function is different from that of the built-in open () function.

The removal of the file needs to be implemented by calling the remove () function. Before deleting a file, it is necessary to determine whether the file exists or not, if so, delete the file; otherwise, nothing will be done.

The following code demonstrates the deletion of the file:

```
01 import os

03 file("rod.txt," "w")

04 if os.path.exists("rod.txt"):

05 os.remove("rod.txt")

[Code Description]
```

Line 3 code creates the file hello.txt

The fourth line of code calls the existing () of os.path module to determine whether the file hello.txt exists.

Line 5 calls remove () to delete the file hello.txt

Renaming Files

The function rename () of the os module can rename files or directories. The following code demonstrates the file renaming operation. If there is a file named hello.txt in the current directory, rename it hi.txt; if there is a hi.txt file, rename it hello.txt.

```
01 # Modify File Name
02 import os
03 li=os.listdir(."")
04 print (li)
05 if "hello.txt" in li:
06 os.rename("hello.txt," "hi.txt")
07 elif "hi.txt" in li:
08 os.rename("hi.txt," "hello.txt")
[Code Description]
```

The third line of code calls listdir () to return the file list of the current directory, where ."'" indicates the current directory.

Opening, Reading and Writing Binary Files

Binary files are any files that are non-text, example of this are images or videos. In working with binary files, we will use the "rb" or "wb" mode. To do that, you must copy a file, a jpeg file to be specific on your desktop and rename it with myimage.jpg. Change the first two lines and edit the program.

```
inputFile = open ('myfile.txt', 'r')

outputFile = open ('myoutputfile.txt', 'w')

to

inputFile = open ('myimage.jpg', 'rb')

outputFile = open ('myoutputimage.jpg', 'wb')
```

Make that you will also change the statement outputFile.write(msg + '\n') back to outputFile. write(msg).

After that, you may now run the program. Always remember that you should have an additional image file that is named as myoutputimage.jpg. on your computer. Take note that when opening the image; the image file should look like myimage.jpg

CHAPTER - 5

USING A FOR LOOP TO WRITE AND READ TEXT FILES

Another important topic to explore when we are working with the Python coding language is the idea of the loop. These are important to a lot of the codes that you will need to write and read, and sometimes, they can help with those conditional statements as well. One of the best things about these loops is that they can get a lot of information into a few lines, which helps to clean up your code and makes it powerful without having to write out a lot of information.

Often, you will start to bring up these loops any time when you are writing out a code where you would like to have a particular program repeat something. Even if it is a few times, this can work as well, but you don't want to mess up the code or waste your time writing that part out a few times. While it may not seem like a big deal to write out that part of the code two or three times to get it to repeat, there could potentially be times when you want to write out the code a hundred times or more. Instead of writing out a hundred lines, or multiple lines a hundred times, you would be able to utilize these loops and get it done in just a few lines. A loop is what you need to handle this work, and you will like how easy and clean it looks.

For example, you may be working on a code, and then you get to a point where you would like to have the numbers listed out from one to ten for you. Of course, this can take up a lot of code and space if you tried to write this out each time you wanted a number listed. But with a loop, you would be able to set it to continue counting up until it reached the conditions that you set ahead of time.

This sounds like it is hard, and as a beginner, you may be worried about how you would be able to do it for yourself. These loops are going to tell your compiler that it needs to repeat the same line or lines of code over and over again until the inserted conditions are met. If you would like to get the code to count from one to ten, then you would tell the compiler that the condition is when the output is higher than ten. Don't worry about this being too confusing; we are going to show you a few examples of how this can work in a moment.

Of course, when you are writing out the loop codes, you must make sure that you put in some condition that will end the loop. Beginners can often forget to set up this condition to end the program, and then they end up in some trouble. The code will keep going through the loop, getting stuck because it doesn't know when it is supposed to stop. You must make sure that you add in a break or a condition to the code so that it knows when it should stop and move on to some of the other things that should be done in the code.

With some of the other methods of traditional coding that we have talked about; or that you may have used in the past, you would have to avoid these loops and write out each line of the code. Even if there were some parts of the code that were similar, or you were retrying the same piece of code to make a pattern show up, this is how a beginner would have to do the work to get it done. This is a tedious process that takes a lot of time, and it is hard to do.

The good news is that you can get these loops and put them to work, ensuring that you can combine a few lines of code and get the compiler to read through it again until conditions are met, rather than having you rewrite the code that many times. This means that instead of writing out potentially hundreds of lines of code, you can write out a few and have the compiler read through it again until it is done.

Each of these loops is going to be helpful and can be used in different circumstances based on what you are trying to get done in the code. The three main types of loops that we are going to explore through the rest of this guidebook include the while loop, the for loop, and the nested loop.

Working with Our While Loop

So, out of the three loops that we can work with, we will start with the while loop in the Python language. The while loop is a good choice to make if you have a predetermined number of times you would like the code to cycle through that line. You can set this up ahead of time, and ensure that the loop goes through it that many times, no more and no less.

When you use the while loop, the goal here is not to allow the code to go through the cycle as many times as it wants, or an indefinite number of times, but you do want to make sure that it goes through five, or six, or however, many times are needed. If you want the program to count from one to ten, for example, then you would set up the loop to do its work ten times. It also makes sure that the loop happens one time, and then checks the conditions before doing it again. With this option, the loop will put the number one on the screen, check the conditions, and then do number two through to ten.

This is a lot to take in and may be hard to understand. The sample code below is a good way to see what the while loop is all about and checks what is going to happen when you try to write it out in your compiler

```
Counter = 1

while(counter <= 3):

principal = int(input("Enter the principal
amount:"))

numberofyeras = int(input("Enter the number
of years:"))

rateofinterest = float(input("Enter the rate of
interest:"))

simpleinterest = principal * numberofyears *
rateofinterest/100

print("Simple interest = %.2f" %simpleinterest)

#increase the counter by 1

counter = counter + 1

print("You have calculated simple interest for 3
time!")
```

Before we move on, take this code and add it to your compiler and let it execute this code. You will see that when this is done, the output is going to come out in a way that the user can place any information that they want into the program. Then the program will do its computations and figure out the interest rates, as well as the final amounts based on whatever numbers the user placed into the system.

With the completed example, we can set up a loop that would go through its iterations three times. This means that the user can get the results they want before the system decides to move on. As the computer programmer, you can go through this and add in more iterations, and have the loop repeat itself more if you want it to base on what is the best option for your program.

Understanding the for Loop

It is going to be a great option any time that you would like to work with a loop, and often it is the only choice that you need. But, there will be some times when this loop is not going to be quite right, and you will need to change it up a little bit. The for loop is the option that you should choose here. This is considered the traditional method for loops so that you can use it in many different situations.

When you bring out the for loop, you have to make sure that it is set up in a way that the user isn't the one that has to provide the program with information on when to stop the loop. Instead, this loop is going to be set up in a way that it goes over the iteration in the order that things show up in the statement. And then, as it reads through the statement, this information is going to show up on the screen. This can nicely work because it isn't going to need any outside force or any outside user to input information in. A good example of how this code is going to loop when you write it out includes:

```
# Measure some strings:

words = ['apple,' 'mango,' 'banana,' 'orange']

for w in words:

print(w, len(w))
```

When you work with the for above loop example, you can add it to your compiler and see what happens when it gets executed. When you do this, the four fruits that come out on your screen will show up in the exact order that you have them written out. If you would like to have them show up in a different order, you can do that, but then you need to go back to your code and rewrite them in the right order, or your chosen order. Once you have then written out in the syntax and they are ready to be executed in the code, you can't make any changes to them.

Opening and Reading Text Files by Buffer Size

There are times that we want to open and read text files by buffer size so that our program will not use much memory resources. And in order to do that, use the read ( ) function which will allow us to specify the amount of buffer size we want.

Try the following program:

```
inputFile = open ('myfile.txt', 'r')
outputFile = open ('myoutputfile.txt', 'w')
msg = inputFile.read(10)
while len(msg):
    outputFile.write(msg)
    msg = inputFile.read(10)
inputFile.close()
outputFile.close()
```

First, we open two files, the inputFile.txt and outputFile.txt files for reading and writing respectively.

Next, we use the statement msg = inputFile. read(10) and a while loop to loop through the file 10 bytes at a time. The value 10 in the parentheses tells the read() function only to read 10 bytes. The while condition while len(msg): checks the length of the variable msg. As long as the length is not zero, the loop will run.

Within the while loop, the statement outputFile. write(msg) writes the message to the output file. After writing the message, the statement msg

= inputFile.read(10) reads the next 10 bytes and keeps doing it until the entire file is read. When that happens, the program closes both files.

When you run the program, a new file myoutputfile.txt will be created. When you open the file, you'll notice that it has the same content as your input file myfile.txt. To prove that only 10 bytes is read at a time, you can change the line outputFile.write(msg) in the program to outputFile.write(msg + '\n'). Now run the program again. myoutputfile.txt now contains lines with at most 10 characters. Here's a segment of what you'll get.

Learn Python in One Day and Learn It Well.

CHAPTER - 6

OBJECT ORIENTED PROGRAMMING

Python is an object-oriented programming language. In fact, most modern languages are. But what exactly does this mean? We've spoken in vague terms of objects and classes but we haven't really established quite what this actually means in in any certain terms one way or another.

An object is an instance of a class. Most things you'll deal with in Python are objects. Earlier, when we worked with file input and output, we created instances of a file class. Every instance has built in methods that it can access that are derived from the class definition itself. So what exactly is a class?

A class is a way of defining objects. This sounds terribly vague, but let's look at it this way.

You likely have or have had a pet, right? Let's say there's a dog, and his name is Roscoe.

Well, Roscoe is an animal. Animals have broad,

generally defined characteristics, but they're all animals, much like Roscoe is an animal. Get comfy with Roscoe, because we're going to be talking him a lot while we talk about the relations between classes and the relations between classes and objects.

We've established that Roscoe is most certainly an animal. He fits the definition of an animal. In this manner, Roscoe is a specific instance of the animal class. If you were writing a simulation of life, and you had people and animals, you would define Roscoe as an instance of animal, just as you declared variable file1 as an instance of file, or you declared tonguetwister as an instance of string.

Now, we need to talk about how we actually define a class and an object within Python.

Create a new file to work with, I'm calling mine pursuitOfRoscoe.py.

Within this file, we're going to start right out the bat by defining a class.

To declare a class, you follow the following template:

```
class name(parent)
```

Let's just make our animal class. Every class which isn't deriving from another class has "object" as its parent, so let's put that.

```
class Animal(object):
```

We're on our way to defining Roscoe, now. We need a way to define an animal. Let's think about what most animals have. Most animals have legs, that's a start. Animals also have Latin names. Let's work with those two. If your class stores data, you generally need to have an initializer function within your class. It's not a necessity, but it is very common practice.

```
class Animal(object):

def __init__(self, legs, name):

self.legs = legs

self.name = name
```

Perfect. Since Roscoe's a dog, he'll have 4 legs, and his species is Canis Lupus Familiaris.

With that in mind, we now have a definition for animal classes that can be used amongst many animals, not just Roscoe. That's the entire idea behind classes: creating reusable data structures for any given object so that the code is more readable, easy to understand, cleaner, and portable, among other buzzword adjectives that are surprisingly very, very true.

How do we declare an instance of this class now? Like anything else!

```
roscoe = Animal(4, "Canis Lupus Familiaris")
```

We can go in and change these variables too. Canis lupus is so formal, and Roscoe's our buddy, so let's change that to Roscoe.

```
roscoe.name = "Roscoe"
```

There we go. Much better.

Hopefully, this makes the distinction between classes and objects much clearer.

Roscoe is a dog, and an animal. Thus he takes from the common concept of being an animal. Since he's an instance of an animal, he automatically receives the traits that all animals have. How cool is that?

Let's go a bit further, and incorporate some functions. What's something that every animal does? Sleep. Every single animal sleeps, aside from Ozzy Osborne.

Let's give animals a function so that they can sleep.

Below our initializer, create a new function called sleep that takes the arguments of self and hours. Then print out a line of text that says the animal's name and how long it's sleeping for. My code ended up looking a bit like this, and hopefully yours will as well.

```
def sleep(self, hours):

print "%s is sleeping for %d hours!" % (self.name, hours)
```

Then below our declaration of Roscoe, let's go ahead and run the "sleep" function with the argument of 4 hours.

```
roscoe = Animal(4, "canis lupus familiaris")

roscoe.name = "Roscoe"

roscoe.sleep(4)
```

Save this and run it. If all goes well, it should print out "Roscoe is sleeping for 4 hours!".

More on Object-Oriented Programming and Classes

There are four primary concepts within object-oriented programming that we need to discuss more in-depth. These are inheritance, polymorphism, abstraction, and encapsulation. Python provides for all of these, and very well at that.

Inheritance is the notion of deriving a class and things from within that class into another child class. There's a very simple way to explain this concept. Classes can break down into other more specific classes. For example, Roscoe is an animal. But he's also a dog. A dog is a type of animal. Shouldn't Roscoe be a dog and not an animal? Isn't he both? How do we handle this?

Think of it this way: every dog is an animal, but not every animal is a dog. So we can break down the animal class even further. The way that we derive one class from another is by inheritance. Here's how we'd declare a dog class which extends the animal class. All dogs have 4 legs aside (for the most part), so we can declare that ahead of time and manually change it if a dog ever doesn't have 4 legs.

```python
class Dog(Animal):

def __init__(self, name):

self.name = name

self.legs = 4
```

The way that this works is that the Dog class is an extension of the Animal class. The Dog class receives all the functions and variables of the dog class, so we don't have to redefine them.

This also means that if we were to erase our first line and re-declare Roscoe more accurately as a dog, we could still declare sleep. Observe.

```
roscoe = Dog("Roscoe")

roscoe.sleep(4)
```

It should go without a hitch. However, the cool thing about child classes is that you can also give them their own functions that their parent can't use. For example, animals don't bark - dogs do. Let's create a bark function in our dog class for practice's sake.

```
def bark(self):

"%s says: Bark!" % self.name

Now let's try to declare bark via Roscoe.

roscoe.bark()
```

It should print out exactly what we entered. To illustrate further, create an instance of parent class Animal, let's call it "lion":

```
lion = Animal(4, "panthera leo")
```

Try to call the method bark by way of Lion.

```
lion.bark()
```

There should be an error. Why is this? Well, it's because - as we said - every dog is an animal, but not every animal is a dog. The bark() function was defined in the Dog class but not in the Animal class, so instances of the Animal class can't access this method at all.

The next concept of object-oriented programming is called "polymorphism". This means that something has the property of being able to perform the same task as something else, but in a different way. There are two ways of achieving this: function overloading (performing a similar function/method but with different parameters) and function overriding (rewriting a function of a parent class so that it works better for your own class).

To illustrate this, let's go back to our bark method. Under our bark method, we're going to create another bark method, declared like this:

```
def bark(number):

print "%s just barked, %d times! How cute." %
(self.name, number)
```

Now we have two different forms of the bark function. If you declare

```
roscoe.bark()
```

You're going to see "Roscoe says: Bark!"

But, if you declare

```
roscoe.bark(3)
```

You'll see "Roscoe just barked, 3 times! How cute."

This is the basic idea of function overloading and polymorphism in essence: giving multiple ways to do a similar thing.

This program is already adorable, but we can make it even more adorable while also learning more about Python coding and string manipulation. Go back to your bark(number) method, and change it so it looks like this:

```
barkString = "Bark! " * number
print "%s just barked, %d times. How cute. %s) (self.name, number, barkString)
```

Now save and run. You can repeat a string multiple times by simply using the multiplication and giving how many times to multiply!

The next major concept of object-oriented programming languages is abstraction. This is the idea of hiding internal details and functionality, to be more forward and more safe for both the programmer and end user. Python shows this by having a very abstract interface compared to other languages and providing a large amount of functionality for you so you never have to get down to the nitty-gritty of what your computer is actually doing behind the scenes.

The last major concept of object-oriented languages is called encapsulation, wherein code and data is wrapped together into a single unit. The primary way that we can display this is by the notion of having a class - not only in Python, but anywhere. Using a class automatically wraps important data and functions together in one easily accessible and usable place. Other datas have something called access control where you can actually dictate what classes can and can't access the data that you're putting in your class. Class data in Python is by default public. All in all, object-oriented programming isn't very tough to grasp, but it's full of concepts that stand for much bigger and larger things, and these are the concepts that can be difficult to understand and implement in the end.

CHAPTER - 7
DATA SCIENCE TIPS AND TRICKS

One of the major strengths of Data Scientists is a strong background in Math and Statistics. Mathematics helps them create complex analytics. Besides this, they also use mathematics to create Machine Learning models and Artificial Intelligence. Similar to software engineering, Data Scientists must interact with the business side.

This involves mastering the domain so that they can draw insights. Data Scientists need to analyze data to help a business, and this calls for some business acumen. Lastly, the results need to be assigned to the business in a way that anyone can understand.

This calls for the ability to verbally and visually communicate advanced results and observations in a manner that a business can understand as well as work on it.

Therefore, it is important for any wannabe Data

Scientists to have knowledge about Data Mining.

Data Mining describes the process where raw data is structured in such a way where one can recognize patterns in the data via mathematical and computational algorithms.

Below are five mining techniques that every data scientist should know:

MapReduce

The modern Data Mining applications need to manage vast amounts of data rapidly. To deal with these applications, one must use a new software stack. Since programming systems can retrieve parallelism from a computing cluster, a software stack has a new file system called a distributed file system.

The system has a larger unit than the disk blocks found in the normal operating system. A distributed file system replicates data to enforce security against media failures.

In addition to such file systems, a higher-level programming system has also been created. This is referred to as MapReduce. It is a form of computing which has been implemented in different systems such as Hadoop and Google's implementation.

You can adopt a MapReduce implementation to control large-scale computations such that it can deal with hardware faults. You only need to write three functions. That is Map and Reduce, and then you can allow the system to control parallel execution and task collaboration.

Distance Measures

The major problem with Data Mining is reviewing data for similar items. An example can be searching for a collection of web pages and discovering duplicate pages. Some of these pages could be plagiarism or pages that have almost identical content but different in content. Other examples can include customers who buy similar products or discover images with similar characteristics.

Distance measure basically refers to a technique that handles this problem. It searches for the nearest neighbors in a higher dimensional space. For every application, it is important to define the meaning of similarity. The most popular definition is the Jaccard Similarity. It refers to the ratio between intersection sets and union. It is the best similarity to reveal textual similarity found in documents and certain behaviors of customers.

For example, when looking for identical documents, there are different instances for this particular example. There might be very many small pieces of one document appearing out of order, more documents for comparisons, and documents that are so large to fit in the main memory.

To handle these issues, there are three important

steps to finding similar documents.

- Shingling: This involves converting documents into sets.

- Min-Hashing: It involves converting a large set into short signatures while maintaining similarity.

- Locality Sensitive Hashing: Concentrate on signature pairs that might be from similar documents.

The most powerful way that you can represent documents assets is to retrieve a set of short strings from the document.

- A k-Shingle refers to any k characters that can show up in a document.

- A min-hash functions on sets.

- Locality-Sensitive Hashing.

Link Analysis

Traditional search engines did not provide accurate search results because of spam vulnerability. However, Google managed to overcome this problem by using the following technique:

- PageRank: It uses simulation. If a user surfing a web page starts from a random page, PageRank attempts to congregate in case it had monitored specific outlines from the page that users are located. This whole process works iteratively meaning pages that have a higher number of users are ranked better than pages without users visiting.

- The content in a page was determined by the specific phrases used in the page and linked with external pages. Although it is easy for a spammer to modify a page that they are administrators, it is very difficult for them to do the same on an external page which they aren't administrators.

In other words, PageRank represents a function which allocates a real number to a web page. The intention is that a page with a higher page rank becomes more important than a page that does not have a page rank. There is no fixed algorithm defined to assign a page rank, but there are of different variety.

For powerfully connected Web Graphs, PageRank applies the principle of transition matrix. This principle is useful for calculating the rank of a page.

To calculate the behavior of a page rank, it simulates the actions of random users on a page.

There are different enhancements that one can make to PageRank. The first one is called Topic-Sensitive PageRank. This type of improvement can weigh certain pages more heavily as a result of their topic. If you are aware of the query in a particular page, then it is possible to be biased on the rank of the page.

Data Streaming

In most of the Data Mining situations, you can't know the whole data set in advance. There are times when data arrives in the form of a stream, and then gets processed immediately before it disappears forever.

Furthermore, the speed at which data arrives very fast, and that makes it hard to store in the active storage. In short, the data is infinite and non-stationary. Stream management, therefore, becomes very important.

In the data stream management system, there is no limit to the number of streams that can fit into a system. Each data stream produces elements at its own time. The elements should then have the same data rates and time in a particular stream.

Streams can be archived into a store, but this will make it impossible to reply to queries from the archival store. This can later be analyzed under individual cases by using a specific retrieval method.

Furthermore, there is a working store where summaries are placed so that one can use to reply to queries. The active store can either be a disk or main memory. It all depends on the speed at which one wants to process the questions. Whichever way, it does not have the right capacity to store data from other streams.

Data streaming has different problems as highlighted below:

- Sampling Data in a Stream

To create a sample of the stream that is used in a class of queries, you must select a set of attributes to be used in a stream. By hashing the key of an incoming stream element, the hash value can be the best to help determine whether all or none of the items in the key belong to the sample.

- Filtering Streams

To accept tuples that fit a specific criterion, accepted tuples should go through a separate process of the stream while the rest of the tuples are eliminated. Bloom filtering is a beautiful technique that one can use to filter streams to allow elements in a given set to pass through while foreign details are deleted.

Members in the selected set are hashed into buckets to form bits. The bits are then set to 1. If you would like to test an element of a stream, you must hash the item into a set of bits using the hash function.

- Count Specific Elements in a Stream

Consider stream elements chosen from a universal set. If you wanted to know the number of unique features that exist in a stream, you might have to count from the start of the stream. Flajolet-Martin is a method which often hashes details to integers, described as binary numbers. By using a lot of the hash functions and integrating these estimates, you finally get a reliable view.

Frequent Item – Set Analysis

The market-basket model features many relationships. On one side, there are items, and on the opposite side, there are baskets. Every basket contains a set of questions. The hypothesis created here is that the number of questions in the basket is always smaller than the total number of items. This means that if you count the items in the basket, it should be high and broad to fit in memory. Here, data is similar to a file that has a series of hoops. In reference to the distributed file system, baskets represent the original file. Each basket is of type "set of items".

As a result, a popular family technique to characterize data depending on the market-basket model is to discover frequent item-sets. These are sets of items that reveal the most baskets.

Market basket analysis was previously applied in supermarket and chain stores. These stores track down the contents of each market basket that a customer brings to the checkout. Items represent products sold by the store while baskets are a set of items found in a single basket.

That said, this same model can be applied in many different data types such as:

Similar concepts: Let items represent words and baskets documents. Therefore, a report or basket has words or things available in the report. If you were to search for words that are repeated in a text, sets would contain the most words.

- Plagiarism: You can let the items represent documents and baskets to be sentenced.

- Properties of Frequent-Item Sets to Know

- Association rules: These refer to implications in case a basket has a specific set of items.

- Monotonicity: One of the most essential properties of item-sets is that if a set is frequent, then all its subsets are numerous.

CHAPTER -8

LOOKING AT MACHINE LEARNING AND HOW THIS FITS IN

While we are on this topic, we need also to spend some time looking at machine learning and how it is able to fit in with the problems of deep learning and our data analysis. Machine learning is another topic that is getting a lot of attention throughout the business world, no matter which industry you spend your time in, and learning how to make this happen, and the importance of machine learning and other parts of artificial intelligence in your project and the models that you create.

When you start diving into all of the advancements that are present with artificial intelligence it sometimes seems a bit overwhelming. But if you are just interested in learning some of the basics for now, you can boil down a lot of the innovations that come with artificial intelligence into two main concepts that are equally as important. These two concepts are going to include the deep learning that we have already spent some time on, and machine learning as well.

These are two terms that have garnered a lot of attention over the years, and because of the buzz that comes with them, it is likely that many business owners assume that these words can be used interchangeably. But there are some key differences that occur between machine learning and deep learning, and it is definitely essential to know the differences and how these two methods relate to each other

With that in mind, we are going to take some time to explore more about machine learning and how it is able to fit into the model that we are creating. There are a lot of examples of both deep learning and machine learning, and we use both of these topics on a regular basis. So, let's dive right in and see a bit more about the differences and similarities between machine learning and deep learning.

What Is Machine Learning?

The first thing that we need to take a look at here is the basics of machine learning. This is going to include a lot of algorithms that are able first to parse the data we have, learn from that data, and then apply what they were able to learn from that data over to make a more informed decision. Basically, it is a process we can use in order to teach our machines and programs on how to learn and make important decisions on their own.

Let's take a look at an example of how this is meant to work. An excellent example of this process would be a streaming service for on-demand music. For this service to stick with some decisions about which artists or songs to recommend to one of their listeners, the algorithms of machine learning will be hard at work. These algorithms are able to associate the preferences of the user with other listeners who have a similar taste in music. This technique, which is often given the generic name of artificial intelligence, is going to be used in many of the other services that are able to offer us recommendations in an automatic manner.

Machine learning is going to fuel all sorts of tasks that are automated and that can span across many industries. This could start out with some firms for data security, who will hunt down malware and turn it off before it infects a lot of computers. And it can go to finance professionals who want to prevent fraud and make sure they are getting the alerts when there are some excellent trades they can rely on.

We are able to take some of the algorithms that come with artificial intelligence and program them in a manner that makes them learn on a constant basis. This is going to be done in a way that stimulates the actions of a virtual personal assistant, and you will find that the algorithms are able to do these jobs very efficiently.

Machine learning is going to be a sophisticated program to work with, and often it takes the right coding language, such as Python, and some of the best libraries out there to get things done. The algorithms that you can create will involve a lot of complex coding and math that can serve as a mechanical function. This function is similar to what we may see a screen on a computer, a car or a flashlight do for us.

When we say that something such as a process or a machine, is able to do "machine learning" this basically means that it's something that is able to perform a function with the data you provide over to it, and then it can also get progressively better at doing that task as time goes on. Think of this as having a flashlight that is able to turn on any time that you say the words "it is dark," so it could recognize the different phrases that have the word dark inside of them, and then knows to continue on with the action at hand.

Now, the way that we can train these machines to do the tricks above, and so much more, can be exciting. And there is no better way to work with this than to add in a bit of neural networking and deep learning to the process to make these results even more prevalent overall.

Machine Learning Vs. Deep Learning

Now we need to take a look at how machine learning and deep learning are going to be the same, and how they can be different. When we look at this in practical terms, deep learning is merely going to be a subset that we see with machine learning. In fact, one reality that we see with this is that deep learning is technically going to be a type of machine learning, and it will function in a manner that is similar. This is why so many people who haven't been able to work with either of these topics may assume that they are the same thing. However, it is essential to understand that the capabilities between deep learning and machine learning are going to be different.

While the basic models that come with machine learning are going to become steadily better what the function you are training them to work with, they are still going to rely on some guidance from you as well. If the algorithm gives you a prediction that is inaccurate, then the engineer has to step in and make sure that the necessary adjustments are done early on. With a model that relies on deep learning though, the algorithm can determine, without any help, whether the prediction that it made is accurate. This is done with the help of a neural network.

Let's go back to the example that we did with the flashlight earlier. You could program this to turn on any time that it can recognize the audible cue of someone when they repeat the word "dark." As it continues to learn, it might then turn on with any phrase that has that word as well. This can be done with just a simple model out of machine learning.

But if we decide to add in a model from deep learning to help us get this done, the flashlight would then be able to turn on with some other cues. Instead of just waiting for the word "dark" to show up, we would see it work when someone said a phrase like "the light switch won't work" or "I can't see" which shows that they are in need of a light right then. A deep learning model is going to be able to learn through its own method of computing, which is going to be a technique that helps the system act in a manner that seems like it has its own brain.

Adding in the Deep Learning to the Process

With this in mind, a model of deep learning is going to be designed in a manner that can continually analyze data with a logic structure, and this is done in a manner that is similar to the way that a human would look at problems and draw conclusions. To help make this happen, the application of deep learning is going to work with an artificial neural network, which is going to be basically a layered structure of algorithms that we can use for learning.

The design of this kind of network can seem a bit confusing in the beginning, but it is designed to work similar to the biological neural network that we see in the human brain. This is an excellent thing for the machine learning and deep learning that you want to do because it can lead us over to a process of knowledge that will be more capable of hard and complicated than what the standard models with machine learning can do.

Of course, there are going to be times when it is tricky to ensure that the model of deep learning isn't going to draw some conclusions that are incorrect. We want it to be able to work on its own to get results, but we have to make sure that we are not getting the wrong answers out of the model. And we need to catch these issues as quickly as possible. If the model is able to continue on and learn the wrong outputs and information, then it is not going to be incorrect the whole time and will not do the work that we want.

Just like with some of the other examples that we are able to use with artificial intelligence, it is going to require a lot of training to make sure that we can see the learning processes turn out the right way. but when this is able to work the way that it should, the functional deep learning is going to be seen ore as a scientific marvel that can be the backbone of true artificial intelligence.

An excellent example that we can look at right now for deep learning is the AlphaGo product from Google. Google worked on creating a computer program that worked with a neural network. In this computer program, the system was able to learn how to play the board game that is known as Go, which is one of those games that needs a lot of intuition and intellect to complete.

This program started out by playing against other professional players of Go, the model was able to learn how to play the game and beat out some of these professionals, beating a level of intelligence in a system that had never been seen before. And all of this was done without the program being told at all when it should make a specific move. A model that followed the standard machine learning requirements would need this guidance. But this program is going to do it all on its own.

CHAPTER -9

LEARN PROGRAMMING WITHIN THE SHORTEST TIME

Do you want to venture into coding, but you have more questions than answers on how to start it? You may be worried about what you need to learn and how to identify bugs as well as fix them. Starting may seem to be a daunting task, but with determination and strong will, you will be able to learn. The good news is, there are plenty of resources online that can help you to master coding. The following are some of our best tips that can set you off on the right foot.

1. Your reasons for learning to code

Before starting, you need to ask yourself why you want to learn to code. Assess the real reasons as to why you want to venture into coding. Do you want to make a career change? Do you want to develop apps? Do you want to start a company for building websites or a tech startup? The answers to these questions will determine which programming languages you need to master and the amount of time you need to learn the language.

Think about your end goal so that you do not find yourself wandering. If you would like to create system software, then you will need to learn C++ along with data structures and algorithms. If you want to shift your career to tech-related fields that require knowledge of coding, then you can attend short-term coding boot camps. You can get useful coding information from interactive tutorials or online courses that you could access free or pay a few dollars.

2. Choose the right programming language

After establishing your end goal for learning how to code, it will be easier for you to know which programming language you will go for. Although all programming languages are functional, some are more user-friendly and easier to learn like HTML, JavaScript, and CSS. These are good if you want to learn how to develop basic websites.

If you want to generate websites that incorporate payment systems and databases, you should consider learning SQL, JavaScript, PHP, and Python. Learning Java can help you in creating android apps. If you want to be flexible and fit in different fields, you can consider learning JavaScript and Python. The good news is that once you learn the basics of programming you can learn any language of your choice, so start with one and learning the rest will be easier for you.

3. Pick a plan on how you will learn

You can decide to take online courses like Udacity or attend coding boot camp classes. You can also learn by yourself using the various tutorials available online. However, the problem with online tutorials is that they are too many that you may get confused in deciding which one is the best. Just pick one and stick to it instead of jumping from one to another. You can take advantage of the free online courses to learn the basics of programming before moving to paid internships for advanced knowledge.

You can also acquire a book that can take you through from the basics to real coding. There are different programming e-books that you can find on the Internet. Most of these books offer good guide practices from project design to debugging code. Interactive tutorials are also useful because they give you examples in action and this makes it easier to understand as a self-taught person. They simplify the coding concepts and give you relevant exercises to tackle before going to another topic.

4. Learn by hands-on coding do not just read

The best way to learn to code is by doing it practically. Once you have learned the basics, you should try to use the knowledge to build something.

You can start by tackling the exercises that come with tutorials or online courses. Therefore, make a project as you continue learning. No matter how much you learn, your coding skills will show in your project.

Use the knowledge you gain or you risk losing it. For example, if you want to develop a website, you can practice using HTML and CSS. Create the underlying HTML codes and run the program. What happens? Modify the systems and see what happens again. Remember practice makes perfect and there is no shortcut in coding. You can start small but think bigger.

Although you may not be the best in the first few weeks, you need to be proud of the small progress that you make and be patient with yourself. Strive to write few code lines that are error-free and logically correct. This is a great achievement for someone new in programming. If you are stuck at some errors, you can Google your errors by copying and pasting the error message with quotation marks on Google search box.

5. Do not ignore the basics

Remember that you cannot run before you learn how to walk! It is particularly important to master the basics of any programming language because the advanced concepts start building from the basics that you have learned. Therefore, you need to put much focus on the basics so that you are not stuck when you reach the back-end programming.

6. Code by hand since it sharpens your proficiency

You should learn to write code on paper then dry run it before transferring it into the computer. Since you would not be able to check if the syntax is correct, you will be concentrating on what you are writing. This method will sharpen your skills in becoming a sound developer. Most job interviews will ask you to write the code on paper.

7. Get a Mentor

Another great way to learn to code is by getting the guidance of an expert. You can ask for help from a person who is good at programming and this will make your learning more comfortable and faster. He/she can help you with code feedback or advice. You can find a mentor online or a local coding meets up.

8. Learn incrementally

You should not try to learn several languages at once, start with the basic ones like HTML then you move gradually to complex ones like PHP, Python or C#. Stay committed, disciplined and focused. After learning something, you can involve someone to look at your project and accept the feedback and improve.

Web Development Projects a Learner Should Begin With

The most excellent way to learn and understand web development is by designing projects. Going through tutorials is not enough if you are not going to implement what you read in them. Therefore, read the tutorials and let those ideas come into reality.

Good projects are those that help you in solving your problems. If you wish to work on projects that will significantly inspire you, we have a list of good projects that you can start with.

1. The quiz app

A beginner can do this excellent project. The app works by requesting you to answer the questions in the app to determine your knowledge on the topic. You can also create this app to test the coding skills of other developers.

User interface

- The user can start by clicking on a button displayed "Take Quiz" or "Start".

- The user then sees a display of multiple-choice questions and the user is supposed to choose one or more answers from the choices given.

- After the user selects the required choices, he/she clicks a button displayed as "Next" until he/she reaches the last page.

- Finally, the user lands on a page that displays the results he/she has gotten from the quiz (passed or failed).

This app can allow the user to create an account where he/she can save the scores. It can also enable the user to add more quizzes to the app.

2. Calculator app

A calculator is a powerful tool since it makes calculations easier for humans. You can use JavaScript to create a calculator app that can solve simple arithmetic calculations like addition, multiplication and division using integers.

User Interface

- The user interacts with a page that shows the current number the user has entered or results from the last calculations.

- The interactive page displays an entry pad that has buttons consisting of numbers 0-9 and operation signs "+", "-", "/", "*", "=", and a "C" button for clear.

- The user can enter numbers by clicking on the names and then click on the arithmetic operator to display the result of the operation.

- The user can click on the "C" button to delete the last number or the previous operation.

3. Christmas Lights

You need to be creative enough to come up with this light display app. You will draw seven-colored circles in a row then you will use a timer to change the intensity of every ring. It works by brightening a colored circle then the next color circle on line goes back to its average strength. This will form a causal sequence of colored lights like the Christmas lights.

User interface

- The user clicks on a button displayed as "START" to start the display or "STOP" to end the show.

- The user can alter the time interval as well as the color intensity and he/she can choose the colors to fill every circle

- The app allows the user to customize the size of the circles, and the number of rows to display.

4. Conversion of Roman Numbers to Decimal Numbers

This app will help you to convert the roman numbers to decimal. You can start with seven symbols and assign them some fixed integer values. For example:

- I can represent number 1 then;

- V = 5

- X=10

- L=50

- C=100

- D=500

- M=1000

The User Interface

- The user is required to enter a roman number into the input field and clicks on the "convert button".

- The result of the roman number converted to decimal number displays on an output field and the user can see it.

- If the user enters a wrong symbol, then the app displays an error message

- The user can convert from decimal to roman and vice-versa

5. To-Do List app

This app can allow you to write down all the things that you want to do and your end goals.

The User Interface

- The user can see a display with an input field where he/she can type the "to-do" item.

- After typing the "to-do" item, the user can click the enter button or submit button then the question is added onto the "to-do" list where the user can see.

- When the user accomplishes a task, he/she should tick against the "to-do" list to show that the job is complete.

- The user can also delete an item by pressing on delete or remove button.

- The user can make changes on the "to-do" list.

- The user can see all the completed tasks as well as those that are active.

- The date of creation of the "to-do" list should also be visible.

- The app saves all the "to-do" items and the updates and it allows the user to retrieve them.

6. Create a Library management system website

This website will automate all the daily work of the library and the website has two sections, the admin's part, and the students/teachers section. Anyone who intends to use the site should register first.

CHAPTER -10

ESSENTIAL LIBRARIES FOR MACHINE LEARNING IN PYTHON

Many developers nowadays prefer the usage of Python in their data analysis. Python is not only applied in data analysis but also statistical techniques. Scientists, especially the ones dealing with data, also prefer using Python in data integration. That's the integration of Webb apps and other environment productions.

The features of Python have helped scientists to use it in Machine Learning. Examples of these qualities include consistent syntax, being flexible and even having a shorter time in development. It also can develop sophisticated models and has engines that could help in predictions.

As a result, Python boasts of having a series or a set of very extensive libraries. Remember, libraries refer to a series of routines and sorts of functions with different languages. Therefore, a robust library can lead to tackling more complex tasks. However, this is possible without writing several code lines again. It is good to note that Machine Learning relies majorly on mathematics. That's mathematical optimization, elements of probability and also statistical data. Therefore, Python comes in with a rich knowledge of performing complex tasks without much involvement.

The following are examples of essential libraries being used in our present.

Scikit – Learn

Scikit learn is one of the best and a trendy library in Machine Learning. It has the ability to supporting learning algorithms, especially unsupervised and supervised ones.

Examples of Scikit learn include the following.

- k-means
- decision trees
- linear and logistic regression
- clustering

This kind of library has major components from NumPy and SciPy. Scikit learn has the power to add algorithms sets that are useful in Machine Learning and also tasks related to data mining. That's, it helps in classification, clustering, and even regression analysis. There are also other tasks that this library can efficiently deliver. A good example includes ensemble methods, feature selection, and more so, data transformation. It is good to understand that the pioneers or experts can easily apply this if at all, they can be able to implement the complex and sophisticated parts of the algorithms.

TensorFlow

It is a form of algorithm which involves deep learning. They are not always necessary, but one good thing about them is their ability to give out correct results when done right. It will also enable you to run your data in a CPU or GPU. That's, you can write data in the Python program, compile it, then run it on your central processing unit. Therefore, this gives you an easy time in performing your analysis. Again, there is no need for having these pieces of information written at C++ or instead of other levels such as CUDA.

TensorFlow uses nodes, especially the multi-layered ones. The nodes perform several tasks within the system, which include employing networks such as artificial neutral, training, and even set up a high volume of datasets. Several search engines such as Google depend on this type of library. One main application of this is the identification of objects. Again, it helps in different Apps that deal with the voice recognition.

Theano

Theano too forms a significant part of Python library. Its vital tasks here are to help with anything related to numerical computation. We can also relate it to NumPy. It plays other roles such as;

- Definition of mathematical expressions

- Assists in the optimization of mathematical calculation

- Promotes the evaluation of expressions related to numerical analysis.

The main objective of Theano is to give out efficient results. It is a faster Python library as it can perform calculations of intensive data up to 100 times. Therefore, it is good to note that Theano works best with GPU as compared to the CPU of a computer. In most industries, the CEO and other personnel use Theano for deep learning. Also, they use it for computing complex and sophisticated tasks. All these became possible due to its processing speed. Due to the expansion of industries with a high demand for data computation techniques, many people are opting for the latest version of this library. Remember, the latest one came to limelight some years back. The new version of Theano, that's, version 1.0.0, had several improvements, interface changes, and composed of new features.

Pandas

Pandas is a library that is very popular and helps in the provision of data structures that are of high level and quality. The data provided here is simple and easy to use. Again, it's intuitive. It is composed of various sophisticated inbuilt methods which make it capable of performing tasks such as grouping and timing analysis. Another function is that it helps in a combination of data and also offering filtering options. Pandas can collect data from other sources such as Excel, CSV, and even SQL databases. It also can manipulate the collected data to undertake its operational roles within the industries. Pandas consist of two structures that enable it to perform its functions correctly. That's Series, which has only one dimension and data frames that boast of two dimensional. The Pandas library has been regarded as the most robust and powerful Python library over the time being. Its primary function is to help in data manipulation. Also, it has the power to export or import a wide range of data. It is applicable in various sectors, such as in the field of Data Science.

- Pandas is useful in the following areas:

- Splitting of data

- Merging of two or more types of data

- Data aggregation

- Selecting or subsetting data

- Data reshaping

Diagrammatic explanations

Series Dimensional

A	7
B	8
C	9
D	3
E	6
F	9

Data Frames dimensional

	A	B	C	D
*0	0	0	0	0
*1	7	8	9	3
*2	14	16	18	6
*3	21	24	27	9
*4	28	32	36	12
*5	35	40	45	15

Applications of pandas in a real-life situation will enable you to perform the following:

- You can quickly delete some columns or even add some texts found within the Dataframe

- It will help you in data conversion

- Pandas can reassure you of getting the misplaced or missing data

- It has a powerful ability, especially in the grouping of other programs according to their functionality.

Matplotlib

This is another sophisticated and helpful data analysis technique that helps in data visualization. Its main objective is to advise the industry where it stands using the various inputs. You will realize that your production goals are meaningless when you fail to share them with different stakeholders. To perform this, Matplotlib comes in handy with the types of computation analysis required. Therefore, it is the only Python library that every scientist, especially the ones dealing with data prefers. This type of library has good looks when it comes to graphics and images. More so, many prefer using it in creating various graphs for data analysis. However, the technological world has completely changed with new advanced libraries flooding the industry.

It is also flexible, and due to this, you are capable of making several graphs that you may need. It only requires a few commands to perform this.

In this Python library, you can create various diverse graphs, charts of all kinds, several histograms, and even scatterplots. You can also make non-Cartesian charts too using the same principle.

Diagrammatic explanations

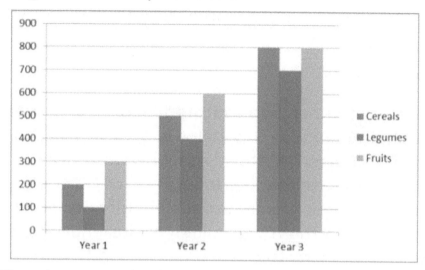

The above graph highlights the overall production of a company within three years. It demonstrates explicitly the usage of Matplotlib in data analysis. By looking at the diagram, you will realize that the production was high as compared to the other two years. Again, the company tends to perform in the production of fruits since it was leading in both years 1 and 2 with a tie in year 3. From the figure, you realize that your work of presentation, representation and even analysis has been made easier as a result of using this library. This Python library will eventually enable you to come up with excellent graphics images, accurate data and much more. With the help of this Python library, you will be able to note down the year your production was high, thus, being in a position to maintain the high productivity season.

It is good to note that this library can export graphics and can change these graphics into PDF, GIF, and so on. In summary, the following tasks can be undertaken with much ease. They include:

- Formation of line plots

- Scattering of plots

- Creations of beautiful bar charts and building up of histograms

- Application of various pie charts within the industry

- Stemming the schemes for data analysis and computations

- Being able to follow up contours plots

- Usage of spectrograms

- Quiver plots creation

Seaborn

Seaborn is also among the popular libraries within the Python category. Its main objective here is to help in visualization. It is important to note that this library borrows its foundation from Matplotlib. Due to its higher level, it is capable of various plots generation such as the production of heat maps, processing of violin plots and also helping in age of time series plots.

Diagrammatic Illustrations

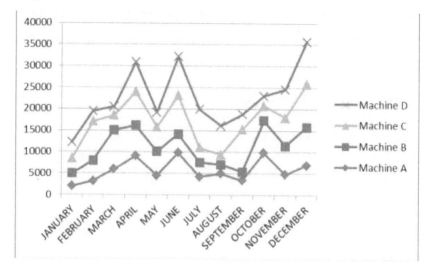

The above line graph clearly shows the performance of different machines the company is using. Following the diagram above, you can eventually deduce and make a conclusion on which devices the company can keep using to get the maximum yield. On most occasions, this evaluation method by the help of the Seaborn library will enable you to predict the exact abilities of your different inputs. Again, this information can help for future reference in the case of purchasing more machines. Seaborn library also has the power to detect the performance of other variable inputs within the company. For example, the number of workers within the company can be easily identified with their corresponding working rate.

NumPy

This is a very widely used Python library. Its features enable it to perform multidimensional array processing. Also, it helps in the matrix processing. However, these are only possible with the help of an extensive collection of mathematical functions. It is important to note that this Python library is highly useful in solving the most significant computations within the scientific sector. Again, NumPy is also applicable in areas such as linear algebra, derivation of random number abilities used within industries and more so Fourier transformation. NumPy is also used by other high-end Python libraries such as TensorFlow for Tensors manipulation. In short, NumPy is mainly for calculations and data storage. You can also export or load data to Python since it has those features that enable it to perform these functions. It is also good to note that this Python library is also known as numerical Python.

SciPy

This is among the most popular library used in our industries today. It boasts of comprising of different modules that are applicable in the optimization sector of data analysis. It also plays a significant role in integration, linear algebra, and other forms of mathematical statistics.

In many cases, it plays a vital role in image manipulation. Manipulation of the image is a process that is widely applicable in day to day activities. Cases of Photoshops and much more are examples of SciPy. Again, many organizations prefer SciPy in their image manipulation, especially the pictures used for presentation. For instance, wildlife society can come up with the description of a cat and then manipulate it using different colors to suit their project. Below is an example that can help you understand this more straightforwardly. The picture has been manipulated:

The original input image was a cat that the wildlife society took. After manipulation and resizing the painting according to our preferences, we get a tinted picture of a cat.

CHAPTER -11
PYTHON DEBUGGING

In some cases, a program is developed, but when running, it does not provide the desired outcome or it gets stuck somewhere in the workflow. This implies that the application should be scrutinized while it is running on a test to get a sense of where the app should be corrected or where things go wrong. This action is what is named by programmers debugging. This task is actively used to make sure that a program is running as it is supposed to be. We will cover this topic and present the commands that are available to debug Python programs. First, let's talk in-depth about what is debugging.

What is debugging?

Debugging is simply the process of finding and fixing errors in a program. Debugging verifies the functioning of a plan to fix statements of operations that make the program stack and not running appropriately. The simplest and most obvious way to debug a program is using the print function in order to spot the output of functions or variables. In general, the print allows getting information to have a look inside of the functioning of the program. However, this method has several drawbacks. The major is that you need to add changes to the code several times in order to add the print in places where you need to extract information. These places are commonly known as breakpoints. Then you have to run the program every time. Some advanced debugger tools can be used. These tools mostly are very efficient and allow saving a great amount of time when used compared to debugging with print.

Python has a debugger that comes by default with the software when installed. This debugger is simply a tool that gives ways to get a look at the code while it is running. When using this tool, you can make changes instantly in the code and alter the values of the variables all while you run the code in chunks. The debugger that comes with Python is named pdb. This tool is in the form of a command-line interface. This debugger, as any package, is imported with the import statement to be able to use it.

import pdb, pdb.set_trace.

To be used, the debugger should be imported into the program you wish to debug. When Python interpreter runs this line, you will be redirected to a prompt command on your terminal in which the program is launched. Typically, this is the prompt of Python with commands that allows you to evaluate your code.

Python Debugger Commands

Python default debugger has several debugging commands which are presented in the table below. Here we cover the most basic one. The first command, list, allows you to list the line where the control workflow is on. You can check specific parts of your code by passing their first and last lines as arguments to the list command. You can also check the code around a specific line bypassing only the number of this line to the list command.

The up and down commands allow navigating around the code of your program. By using these commands, you can know which statement is calling the function that is currently running or understand reasons why the interpreter is behaving or running certain code parts. The next and step are commands that allow resuming execution of the code line by line. The next command will jump to the following line of the function that is currently running even if it calls another function. On the contrary, the step function allows you to go deeper in the code chain rather than just executing the following line. Finally, the break is a command that enables adding new breakpoints with no requirements to make any modifications in the source code.

List Python debugger commands

Debug command	Explanation
Alias or a	allows creating an alias to the command
args or rgs	allows showing the list of arguments
break or b	allows setting breakpoints.
disable	allows disabling breakpoints supplied as a list separated by a space
ignore	allows setting a count for several breakpoints
commands	allows specifying a command list for several breakpoints
continue or c or cont	continue running the code until it reaches a breakpoint
exit	quit the debugger
interact	launch an interactive interpreter
list or l	allows showing the code for specific lines

next or n	resumes execution until the following line of the function currently running
restart	allows restarting the program
step or s	run expression in the current line
unalias	removes alias
where or w	displays a trace of the recent last frame
down or d	goes to the next line down
up or you	goes to the above line
clear or cl	allows clearing all breakpoints
enable	allows enabling breakpoints
condition	allows setting conditions for breakpoints as a test that should be evaluated to true to set the breakpoint
p	allows evaluating the expression in the current line

help or h	If no argument is supplied, displays list of commands, otherwise, displays information about the command passed as an argument
jump or j	allows setting the number of the line to run next; it allows jumping code parts or running the code from the start
longlist or ll	allows showing the whole code for the function currently running
quit or q	exit the debugger and abort the program
return or r	continue running the code until hits a function return
tbreak	allows making a temporary breakpoint
until or ill	if no argument is passed, it continues running the code until a line which has a number superior to the current is reached

whatis	displays the expression type

Now that you know the concept behind debugging and its basic commands, let's see a real example. We consider the following code saved in a file named test.py.

```python
def Myfct1 (A):

print ('A by 2 is:', A * 2)

return A * 2

def Myfct2 (B, A):

C = B * A

A = 4

B = 'name'

Myfct2 (B, A)
```

You can notice that this code does not import Python debugger, the pdb module. Instead, we are going to launch the function in the prompt with Python in a debugger mode with the following command:

```
C:\Users\***\Desktop>Python -m pdb test.py
```

```
> c:\users\***\desktop\test.py(1)<module>()

-> def Myfct (A):

(Pdb)
```

As you can see, Python did not return the usual >>> in the prompt but it returned instead (Pdb). This means that the debugger is waiting for debugger commands. Now, let's test some of the commands listed in Table 9 above to get a sense of how the debugger works. We start by the list command.

```
(Pdb) list

1 -> def Myfct1(A):

2 print ('A by 2 is:', A * 2)

3 return A * 2

4

5 def Myfct2(B, A):

6 C = B * A

7

8 A = 4

9 B = 'name'

10 Myfct2(B, A)
```

```
[EOF]
```

In this example, we applied the list command with no argument. It returned the content of the file with line numbers. If we pass arguments (i.e. line numbers) to the list command, it will return only the code that shows between these lines. For instance:

```
(Pdb) list 2, 3

 2 print ('A by 2 is:', A * 2)

 3 return A * 2

(Pdb)
```

If we use now the next command it will return, the next line after where the current curser is:

```
(Pdb) next

> c:\users\***\desktop\test.py(5)<module>()

-> def Myfct2(B, A):

(Pdb)
```

We skip lines in the debugger using the jump command as follows:

```
(Pdb) jump 8

> c:\users\*****\desktop\test.py(8)<module>()

-> A = 4

(Pdb)
```

If we try to print the variable 'A', Python will display a name error because this statement is not yet executed. The curser is just pointing to this line:

```
(Pdb) A

*** NameError: name 'A' is not defined

(Pdb)
```

Now, in order to print variable names, we should run the program with commands that run the program not just show its content. Among these commands is the continue command. So, let's run now the continue command:

```
(Pdb) continue
```

Traceback (most recent call last):

```
File "C:\Users\****\Anaconda3\lib\pdb.py", line
1697, in main

 pdb._runscript(mainpyfile)

 File "C:\Users\****\Anaconda3\lib\pdb.py", line
1566, in _runscript

 self.run(statement)

 File "C:\Users\****\Anaconda3\lib\bdb.py", line
585, in run

 exec (cmd, globals, locals)

 File "<string>", line 1, in <module>

 File "c:\users\****\desktop\test.py", line 8, in
<module>

 A = 4

 NameError: name 'Myfct2' is not defined
```

Uncaught exception. Entering post mortem debugging

Running 'cont' or 'step' will restart the program

```
 > c:\users\*****\desktop\test.py(8)<module>()

 -> A = 4
```

```
> c:\users\*****\desktop\test.py(8)<module>()

-> A = 4
```

Now, here that the continue launched different built-in functions of the debugger. It finally displayed an Error name for the 'Myfct2' because the 'def' statement of this function was not executed. Now, if we try to print the value of the variable ' A ', we get:

```
(Pdb) A

4

(Pdb)
```

If we reach the bottom of the file and run, for instance, the next command, Python debugger returns:

```
(Pdb) next
```

Post mortem debugger finished. The test.py will be restarted

```
> c:\users\***\desktop\test.py(1)<module>()
```

```
-> def Myfct1(A):
```

The longlist command allows showing the entire code. For instance:

```
(Pdb) longlist

1 -> def Myfct1 (A):

2 print ('A by 2 is:', A*2)

3 return A * 2

4

5 def Myfct2 (B, A):

6 C = B * A

7

8 A = 4

9 B = 'name'

10 Myfct2(B, A)

(Pdb)
```

Now, to run a code, we use the command step. For instance, let's quit the debugger with the command q() and restarted it again to test the command step.

```
 (Pdb) q()

C:\Users\****\Desktop>Python -m pdb test.py

> c:\users\****\desktop\test.py(1)<module>()

-> def Myfct1 (A):

(Pdb) step

> c:\users\****\desktop\test.py(5)<module>()

-> def Myfct2 (B, A):

(Pdb)
```

As you can notice, when a step command is run, the current line is def Myfct2 (B, A). This means that it is executed the 'def' statement of the first function. We can test that by calling this function:

```
(Pdb) Myfct1 (3)

A by 2 is: 6

6

(Pdb)
```

We can also pass an argument to step function to specify which line to run. For instance, we pass as argument Line 8. The debugger will run everything before line 8.

As we can see from the example below, we can both print the variable A and call the function Myfct2 because these statements were both executed.

```
(Pdb) step 8

> c:\users\****\desktop\test.py(8)<module>()

-> B = 'name'

(Pdb) A

4

 (Pdb) Myfct2 (5, 3)

(Pdb)
```

Because we have reached the end of the file, let's use continue to go back to the beginning of the file and test other commands.

```
(Pdb) cont

The program finished and will be restarted

> c:\users\****\desktop\test.py(1)<module>()

-> def Myfct1 (A):
```

As you can see when running continue command at the end file, the debugger shows a message that lets you know that the program has finished and it is restarting. Now, we are going to test the whatis command:

```
(Pdb) whatis 2

<class 'int'>

(Pdb)
```

This command returns the type of the data object of the expression that appears in the Line passed as an argument.

CONCLUSION

Congratulations on finishing this book, let's hope it was informative and able to provide you with all of the tools you need to achieve your goals whatever they may be.

Working in Python can be one of the best programming languages for you to choose. There are just so many things that you can do with the Python program, and since you are able to mix it in with some of the other programming languages, there is almost nothing that you can't do with Python on your side. It is not a problem if you are really limited on what you are able to do when using a programming language. Python is a great way for you to use in order to get familiar and to do some amazing things without having to get scared at how all the code will look. For some people, half the fear of using a programming language is the fact that it is hard to look at with all the brackets and the other issues. But this is not an issue when it comes to using Python because the language has been cleaned up to help everyone read and look at it together.

This guidebook has given you all the tools that you need to hit the more advanced parts of Python. Whether you are looking at this book because you have a bit of experience using Python and you want to do a few more advanced things, or you are starting as a beginner, you are sure to find the answers that you need in no time. So look through this guidebook and find out everything that you need to know to get some great codes while using the Python programming.

The next step is to get started with the basics of programming in Python. You will find that even as a beginner or someone who has never done any kind of coding in the past, working with the Python language is easy enough to learn. And we spent some time in this guidebook learning more about how this is going to work, and how we can code in no time.

There are a lot of reasons why people and businesses are going to want to learn how to work with the Python language, and with some of the codes and more that we looked at in this guidebook will show us just how easy working with this kind of language can be overall. It is one of the best coding languages for basic coding all the way up to data analysis and machine learning, so there is always going to be a lot of things that you are able to do with it.

This guidebook took some time to explore more about what Python is able to do for us. We looked at some of the basics, like how to install this language on your computer, and then moved on to some of the different codes that you can write out with the help of this language. And then, we moved on to how we can use this more practically with the help of a good data analysis to push it along and help your business learn from the data and everything it has been able to do overtime.

When it is time for us to explore more about Python programming and what we can do with some simple coding along the way, make sure to read through this guidebook and learn how to get started.

Well, you don't need to be proficient in Python to conduct data analysis in Python. All you need to do is to master five Python libraries to effectively find a solution to a wide array of data analysis problems. So, you need to start learning these libraries one by one. Remember that you don't have to be a pro at building great software in Python to conduct data analysis productively.

Don't forget, Numpy. This is another powerful Python package useful for scientific calculation. Having the correct understanding of Numpy will allow you to use tools such as Pandas. Remember,

Pandas feature advanced data structures and manipulation tools to simplify data analysis.

That said, one thing that you should avoid doing is trying to learn every tool and library in Python at the same time. When you attempt to learn everything at once, you will spend a lot of time-shifting between different concepts, properties, and getting frustrated, and switching to something else.

So, you should try to concentrate on the following basic steps:

- Master python basics

- Master Numpy

- Learn Pandas

- Understand Matplotlib

From here, you can continue to expand on more topics.

I hope you have learned something!

Lightning Source UK Ltd.
Milton Keynes UK
UKHW022008091220
374896UK00010B/683